MW00906676

Prophet Margins –

Poems and Prayers

by John Freal

2019

If you write poetry, it's your own fault.

Cover: Grand Canyon from the South Rim

Prophet Margins - Poems and Prayers

Copyright 2019 by John E. Freal. All right reserved.

Portions of the text, up to 10%, may be quoted in any form without written permission.

Library of Congress Control Number: 2019919275

ISBN: 9780578610382

Contents

An Introduction

As a college student I witnessed a conversation between two friends - history and political science majors - in which they were talking about some big idea. I don't remember exactly what it was, but one of them said, "Well Marx says this about that." And the other responded, "What about Hegel's idea?" Then the first said just, "Freud." To which his friend replied, "Jung and Kierkegaard before that." I had no idea what they meant by all this. Perhaps it was just nonsense. But I was fascinated by the idea that something wonderful or grand or meaningful could be expressed in just a few words. Haiku can be like that.

So what is haiku besides something with 17 syllables? It developed from renga, a form of collaborative poetry which began in 15th century Japan. The first stanza of a renga, called the hokku, was limited to 17 syllables. Then the next poet wrote a stanza with 14 syllables, and then the third stanza had 17 syllables again. The renga could continue like this for many stanzas, each limited in the number of syllables and required to connect to something in the stanza before it. The rules made the collaborative process fair and whole and also rather elaborate. Haiku developed as the collaborative gatherings of poets became less frequent.

Haiku are at least for me a making or a work rather than art. This is not to say that they can't be art. Great poets have written haiku. As I wondered what might be a definition of haiku - a kind of superword or definition or micromeme - the first two lines of this haiku appeared (A definition of a word not yet spoken). And in writing this I have discovered that superword and micromeme are not recognized words. So these words might also be definitions of haiku - even though they don't have 17 syllables. Should the definition of haiku be a haiku, a search, and a discovery? When haiku work, they are like a coiled piece of DNA, uncoiling to reveal much more than 17 syllables. They can be a source of mystery that laughs at the literal and riddles with many answers or none.

I was reading some of these haiku to a writers' group some months ago when a friend told me that he liked them but wished I had slowed way down. I had no sooner finished one haiku when another one was taking him in a new direction, perhaps a kind of poetic whiplash. So there are photographs included to get you, dear reader, to slow down. They may or may not have something to do with the poetry. Their function is to get you to cast about.

Cast is good word,
Not yet corrupted or overused.
One can forecast or be downcast.
One can have a certain cast of mind
Or cast a horoscope.
Cast your bread upon the waters.
Cast your fate to the wind.
For his tunic they cast lots.
Ideas can be cast in stone.
Spells can be cast.
We can cast a shadow,
Cast doubt, cast out,
Cast aspersions, cast off, cast down,
Cast aside, cast adrift, and cast ashore.
Cast about might refer to throwing things around,
But the meaning here is to look around, seek, figure
out –
See other lives and open your own life
For a new glimpse too.
Perhaps know as you are known.
Lay plans; go figure; cast about.

The title, *Prophet Margins*, besides being a play on
words, is a hope for change of heart. Change often
happens at the margins. For example, in economics
and probability marginal variables are ones that
measure change. If prophets are doing the changes,
perhaps hearts can be changed.

Imaginings of the Prophets

Haiku

A definition
of a word not yet spoken,
haiku open hearts.

Temple of Spirit,
form to be felt, seen and touched,
mirror of the soul,

sign of invisible grace,
the body is a sacrament.
                    - from John O'Donohue

Be still and still move.
The whole world is our cloister.
The world is holy.
                    - from Saint Francis Of Assisi

Beatitudes

Blest are the empty,
those with nothing more to lose.
Theirs is the kingdom.

> We are open for healing,
> vulnerable in mourning.

Blest are the gentled.
For the love they give they will
inherit the earth.

> Our hearts hunger for presence.
> You fill our yearnings with love.

Blest those who receive.
Blest too are the merciful.
Blessings go both ways.

> Blest is the heart that is whole,
> the vision that is open.

Peacemakers - children of God,
compassion in human form,
healing for the world

> The path of our suffering
> is the way to our freedom.

Several years ago I wrote a haiku for each of the 150 biblical Psalms and published them as *Poor Poet's Psalter*. In this section I am taking the words of writers who have become prophets for me and rewritten them as haiku or renga. Though various people are given credit for their ideas, none of them are direct quotes.

Try to understand
Because the work of the heart
Is never complete
                    - from Muhammad Ali

Unless we agree
to suffer we will never
escape suffering.
                    - from DT Suzuki

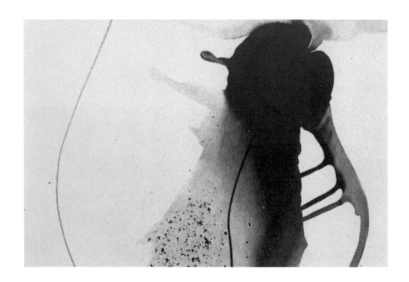

The temple of God
is the soul of each person;
God is within you.
                    - Saint Paul's essential insight

Our work is to be
open to all the fullness
poured into our hearts.
                    - from Rowan Williams

Let us love others,
not just in word or speech but
in truth and action.
                    - 1 John 3:18

The spark we call soul
wants the One who shares our self,
our own share of grace.
          - Saint Augustine's insight

You are so easy
to come to that even grass,
water bear witness.

Your mercy lets me water
my sitting place with teardrops.   Psalm 6:7
                                   - from Thomas Merton

The totality
of our presence can become
a flame of wholeness.

Lighting a flame from a flame
we have another wholeness.
                              - from St. Symeon, the New Theologian

Your beliefs will be
the light by which you see, but
they will not be what

you do see, and they will not
substitute for your seeing.
                                   - from Flannery O'Connor

A revolution,
another intensity,
holy is not soft.

Holiness is a furnace
transforming all who enter.

This symphony is
a fusion of simple and
complex - Isaiah.

His name means God's salvation.
He brings judgement, comfort, hope.

- from Eugene Peterson, Introduction to Isaiah

Receive the Holy.
Then Christ spoke of forgiveness.
We breathe the same air.

- John 20:22-23

The Word was with God.
The light shines in the darkness.
All receive the light.
                    - from John's Prologue

Through fire and ice
deep hope flows over deep time.
Build our sense of scale
                    - from Teilhard

The place Jesus takes
in our soul he will not leave
He loves to dwell there
                - from Lady Julian of Norwich (1342-1416)

Our incarnation -
the celebrant reminds us,
this is my body.

God's Spirit resides in us.
How will I be Jesus now?
                        - from Father Richard Rohr

Blindness

When you lie about
that which is, you do not thirst
for that which should be

- from Nietzsche and John 8:44

Vision

Image and likeness
already children of God
made by love to love

- from Genesis 1:26, 1 John 3:2, and Fr. Richard Rohr

Waking

Waking from a dream
of angels, I knew that You
were here all along.

My days pass in your presence.
Teach me how to number them.
                    - from Psalm 90

Wondering

Who are humans that
you care and crown us with your
luminous presence?
                    - from Psalm 8

May incarnation,
God with a human face, find
its place in our hearts

- from Father Richard Rohr

The Spirit of I am
is on me and a blessing
to bring the good news,

to heal the broken-hearted,
and speak for the captives.

- Jesus, Luke 4 and Isaiah 61

Don't give yourself to
what is finite or strip your
soul of its beauty.
                        - Psalm 81

Time is really the
information that we don't have.
Time's our ignorance.

Where did our yesterdays go?
What machine detects the soul?
                - from Carlo Rovelli and Ramon Panikkar

In the unfruitful
works of darkness take no part;
Instead expose them.
                        - Ephesians 5:11

All creation groans.
God is with us and for us
in our suffering.

Trust death and resurrection.
There is light in darkness.

- from Father Richard Rohr

God brings death to life
and calls into being what
does not yet exist.

- from Romans 4:17

Come awake to the
mystery of being here.
Enter your presence.

- from John O'Donohue

Journey from a life
of religious culture to
one centered in God,

from the bondage of self to
the freedom of forgetting
                              - from Marcus Borg

A word of God is
what I am. I can't change that
nor do I want to.
                              - from Alice Walker

Trinity in Genesis

In the beginning
God created, the Spirit
hovered, there was light.

                    - from Genesis 1:1-3

Presence and power
can be seen through the beauty
of God's creation

                    - from Romans 1:20

Let us make humans
in our image and likeness
… and so it happened.

                    - from Genesis 1:26-30

I am going to
prepare a place for you so
you may be with me.

- from John 14:3

All creation is
a manifestation of
God in space and time.

- from Romans 1:20

The goal is sharing
the life of the Trinity,
for both Christ and us.

- from Duns Scotus

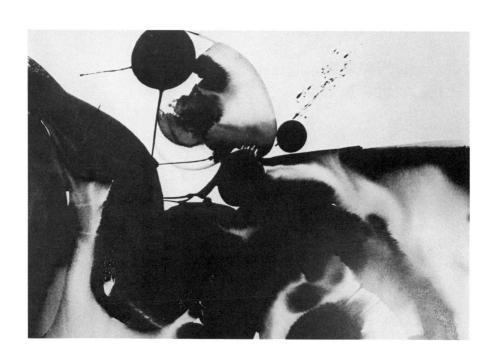

Leaders without care,
each looking after his own,
they go their own way.

The upright humans perish,
and no one cares for the poor.

                    - from Isaiah 56-57

Too many view God
as one who excludes those who
don't get "his" name right.

How could you trust such a small
God or feel loved and free?

                    - from Richard Rohr

I am not afraid
of your pain. I have wept too.
I am your brother.

                    from Henri Nouwen

Beauty of the world -
Christ's tender smile for us
coming through matter
                    -from Simone Weil

God sang to the world,
"I am made whole by your life.
Each soul completes me."
                    - Hafiz

Be gracious to me
for I am lonely. My heart
and soul are troubled.

- from Psalm 25

The last connection
the dying have with the world
appears to be love.

Death becomes a time of growth.
Love pours in and out of us.

- from Kathleen Dowling Singh

Reach to a fullness
we can't imagine from this
side of the process.

- from Thomas Keating

I sense your presence,
growing ever more intense
everywhere I am.

- from Teilhard

Pray without ceasing.
Rejoice always; give thanks in
all circumstances.

Let the Spirit move in you
for this is the will of God.

                              - 1 Thesselonians 5

I will place my law
within them, and I will write
it upon their hearts.

                              - Jeremiah 31:31-33

This is how you loved
so everyone might have life:
You gave us the Christ.

                              - John 3:16

I arise today
with your wisdom to guide me
over earth and sea.

- from St. Patrick

Let anyone come.
Outsiders seeking justice
shall find salvation.

- from Isaiah 56

They cling to their hates
else sensing they must begin
to deal with their pain.

- James Baldwin

The Prophets

Their voice gives wisdom
and courage and then invites
imagination.

-from Walter Brueggemann

The End

It all will be well
in the end. If it's not well,
it's not yet the end.

-from the Best Exotic Marigold Hotel

Gates of Paradox

I can listen from my little ego self or from my thinking mind or from my praying heart. Paradox can help me get past the first two and help me find the heart. Or as it says in 1Corinthians 2, the Spirit explores the depths of everything. The small self has no room for the gifts of the Spirit. To that part of us they seem folly and cannot be recognized. Yet our souls can assess their value because we have the Spirit of Christ.

A Short Course in Being

Abide in love. That's
enough for life to flow now
and forevermore.

Between One and Two

I am not the earth
or God or you, yet I am
not other either.

Freedom?

Being merely right
does little to bring beauty
or love to the world.

We often think of freedom as being able to say or do what
we want. But that is usually just getting pushed around by
our egos. Freedom is something more. How should we act in
freedom and love?

The Word of God

The word is near you
in your mouth and in your heart;
can't plead ignorance.

God's will is no mystery.
Revelation waits for you.

Thresholds

The courage to step
across a new threshold will
lead to broken hearts.

I am blessed and then broken,
just like the bread that we share.

Vocation

The work is not done
until our churches become
field hospitals.

Seeing that world become whole,
we will be free to come home.

In Praise of Paradox

Merely the threat of
infinity explodes
either/or thinking.

I will allow myself to
embrace the ambiguous.

Paradox belongs;
darkness and light coexist;
death is part of life.

Sacred space can feel strange;
freedom takes getting used to.

Idle Worship   (spelled like this on purpose)

Fulfill the law by
totems, temples and rules?
Trade them all for love.

Searching

Hold this truth lightly -
through giving up certainty
we find happiness.

Begin

Faith begins with this -
the heart is vulnerable
when it is open.

Where the Light Shines

Risk living through trust.
Though the path behind is lit,
ahead is darkness.

Lost and Found

The world around me
is both your revelation
and your hiding place.

Liminal Threshold

When I'm in trouble,
keep the pain until learning
what it has to teach.

Pain not transformed is passed on.
God is also suffering.

Unhealthy

No need for small self.
Jesus exposed the lie that
the system saves us.

The journey may take a while;
we may even lose our baggage.

Soul 1 (Ego 0)

Break free from the lie
that we are separate from God.
Though we are broken

vessels, God fills us with life,
this gift the ground of being.

∃ (There exists)

Let my prayer become
a silence in the ocean
of being - YHWH

Prayer Wheel

Gaze turned inside out -
approach this geometry
with humility.

I do not know where to go,
or where I can even start.

Untitled

When truth transcends our
logic, it can only be
grasped through paradox.

Journey

When things fall apart,
enter by the narrow gate.
Hard roads lead to life.

Say yes to trails of tears.
Grace travels along these ways.

Creation

To resist evil
find goodness in the heart
of God's creation.

All beings have God's Spirit.
Proceed without violence.

Blindness and Vision

Through a glass darkly
I find where to live and move
and have my being

Among Other Things

Jesus came to show
this pattern of life and death
and resurrection.

Faith

On a dark journey
I'm asked again, "Are you sure?"
"No, but I have faith."

Mercy

If I am always
in need of mercy, I will
never stop growing.

Works

In practice if I
do not do, I have not heard
and do not believe.

Sadness

Receive this moment
of sadness as the presence
of Christ within you.

Prayer

A way of trusting,
living and delighting in
the presence of God

Limits of Language

The Tao that can be
told is not the eternal
Tao for anyone.

Islam

Peace from submission -
all the rivers of the world
run into the sea.

Answers

What I seek is what
I find, and how I get there
is where I arrive.

Letting Go

I let go of what
I thought I knew to find truth
I never dreamed of.

Alive and Well

A Retirement Discovery

In the end I will
lose control even though I
need not wait till then.

Danger

Ideology -
A stale substitute for
what God has for me.

It promotes the illusion
of separation from God.

Feeling Full

Enough to do here.
To be is often enough
to keep me flying.

Flow #1

Don't store it up.
Divine love is infinite.
Give it all away.

Flow #2

My vibrations found
prayer happened, and I was there,
made whole for a time.

Gift of Tears

A basis for hope
in Christ and for history
life instead of death.

Thank you for the joy
found when your light flows through me.

Inside Out

We follow your call.
Our prayer makes us all healers,
inside turning out.

Outside In

Hold your truth lightly;
Trust transcendent presence,
outside coming in.

Time's Arrow

I shall avoid that
in the future since I can't
change that in the past.

Fear Not

Outcomes are often
more merciful and grace-filled
than what we hoped for.

Legacy

Our faith can become
a generous way of life,
creative chaos.

It might be better to be
disorganized religion.

Art and Science

I went on plodding,
rewarded by the beauty,
toward the unexpected.

From a Creed

We move in history, in time,
honoring those who came before,
hoping in our children,
building on what we love
for a world of meaning and hope,
bearing the burden and the grace,
and looking for the prophetic.

Rhythm

In love and freedom
from the beginning I can
choose these waves of prayer.

Wonderful imagery shines;
light flows because it's so light.

A Kind of Understanding

Amazing to me
that sometimes I see the bones,
structure with no words.

Art's intention is to take
us to heaven for a time.

Standard

The standard linkage
is if…then…but and so what.
All the rest comes hard,

and sometimes we need a rest,
a grace if we look for it.

Where and Who

The place where I am
already I can't enter
since I'm there now.

I'm lost in the universe;
I am a child of God.

Finding Faith

My beliefs may be
a light which helps me see, but
they are not my faith.

Words and images cannot
replace my experience.

Varieties of Knowing

Sometimes I wonder what I know.
Like you, I have opinions.
And if you don't like them,
there are others from my minions.

The sun comes up and runs its course
with other certainties in kind
that most times I hold lightly now
and pay them little mind.

Beliefs can be just what I want,
and what I wanted once seemed clear.
But the light of belief became a shadow,
and shadows fade and disappear.

Though wants and facts attend me still,
in presence now I find I grow.
With here and this my seeing leans.
The ground of love and trust I know.

Untitled

A praying mind brings
my presence to the sacred
in all creation.

Recovering

I left the garden
when very young. Now I am
beginning again.

Lesson One
(one of the first questions in the Baltimore Catechism)

God is not "out there,"
but in me, in you, in them.
God is everywhere.

Learned this when we were children;
often forgot as adults.

Good Morning

Held by the beauty
at daybreak, I stood for a
time on holy ground.

Sacramental universe
Epiphanies everywhere

Our Work

Our work is to be
a light, to live this shining
truth as best we can -

an alternative way to
understand humility.

Here Not There

Caesar is not Lord.
Neither are all our little
Caesar principles.

The evacuation plan
is just not going to work.

For Josh and Bertha

He only says yes
and thank you; she holds his hand
and reads him Scripture.

He walks better now and learns
to say no to the nurses.

Second Coming

Our Christ is the light
that allows us to see things
in all their fullness.

Awe

The fear of the Lord
opens me up to beauty
in the universe.

Let Beauty Fill Us

The universe is
an immense artwork to which
we can contribute.

Rejoice in the universe;
participate in the art.

A Short Psalm

Always your presence
is before me ~ the earth is
full of your glory.

No Privacy Here

Can not continue
to think of our salvation
as merely private.

You Are What You Eat or Communion

A mime in 4 acts
is memory and mystery ~
give thanks, break, take, eat

Calling

We share the call to
be the revelation of
God's love in the world.

How does that activity
manifest the love of God?

Before Words

The attitude that
precedes saying anything
is really a prayer.

Flow #1

We are created
to share in the flow of love
from the Trinity.

Flow #2

We flow into God.
It is love's nature to flow.
God flows into us.

The Way

The great commandment
was learned in community,
led to mended lives.

Lent #1

I come to renew
my own "yes" to the work and
play of Christ in us.

Lent #2

It's time to make friends
with my failings and honor
my contradictions.

Lent #3

I'm invited to
forget myself on purpose
and join in the dance.

One

You said that there is
only one suffering, and
it belongs to God.

There is only one love too,
and it is the love of God.

Most of us do not
see things as they are - we
see them as we are

Isaiah III

We really don't know
about what has been prepared
for those who love God.

Christ at Daybreak

I stand on the earth.
Let me breathe in your presence
and breathe out your peace.

Nonviolence

Forgive everything.
Resist all forms of evil.
Love God; love others

Find justice through suffering.
Look for beauty – glimpse the truth.

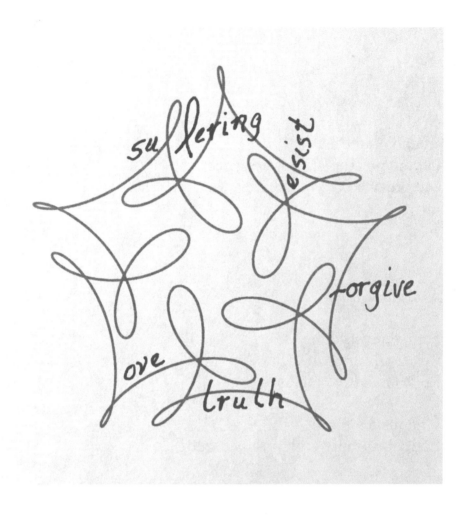

The preceding renga and the words in the image above are from Gandhi's definition of nonviolence. It is not a precise definition but broadly conceptual. The five-fold graph is a function in the complex plane. It would not be visible without its real and imaginary parts.

Excuse Me, Did You Drop This?

Limits

Haiku can be odd.
This one keeps fighting itself.
Please ignore these lines.

Traffic

You don't have to be
a dumb ass to drive like that,
but it no doubt helps.

Miss Placed

She said, "Ladies with
copper bottoms would have to
scrub them no longer."

Beginning of Conspiracy Theory

Chicken Little said,
"The sky is falling; a piece
just hit me today."

Not Noticed

They were beyond lost,
like fish passing in the night
their focus inward.

A Sermon

A psalm of hubris
was the theme of the message
whose end was welcomed.

Not Worth Discussing

I shall not mention
his compassion or morals
or his truthfulness.

Not Original

Original sin
is not biblical; it is
Augustinian.

Bloviators

What suffering or
experience claims for you
the crown of wisdom?

By Their Fruit

Fundamentalists
use the yeast of the Pharisees.
Their bread comes out flat.

Delight in what is alive
in the rhythm of the Word.

Worthy

I hope that I'm not
using my faith to be just
incredibly trite.

Brush Up Your Shakespeare

Today it may be
foul or fair ~ the Ides of March
has come. Be aware.

Don't Step in It

Dogma is doctrine
literalized and turned
to idolatry.

A Pleasure to Serve

Mystic to vendor:
"Make me one with everything."
Vendor to mystic:

"I can't; you are already,
but would you like a hot dog?"

Talking with the Mind Full

They have talked to God
but give no evidence of
listening to him.

Birthday Wishes

The heavens rejoice;
the whole earth is glad for you,
that you are alive.

I echo that gladness with
this blessing on your birthday.

Fall Colors

Falling in autumn
~ life in the Spirit for the
second half of leaf.

Before Surgery

(This haiku was originally about making the ego small so the Spirit could grow, but it's also appropriate for hip surgery.)

This container must
stretch or die and be replaced
by something better.

After Surgery

Surgery went well,
and the pain is not too bad.
Thanks for your kindness.

Crossings

Cross #1

Releasing control,
security, and esteem is
the way of the cross.

Not many of us follow
this way. We wander elsewhere.

Cross #2

Like modern vaccines
the cross lifted up becomes
a source of healing.

Cross #3

Thought the journey might
be easy until struck by
the left hand of God.

Cross #4

Following Jesus
through a path of suffering
becomes our great joy.

Cross #5

Blind to the cross that
invites us to suffering
then delivers us

Cross #6 from Richard Rohr

Life accepting death,
can we follow Jesus' way,
the way of the cross?

What life in Christ means is that
the way down is the way up.

Cross #7

Be vulnerable.
The cross redefines success;
our woundedness wins.

Cross #8 from Richard Rohr

The cross was a gift
so we could witness God's love
in dramatic form.

With Us

Jesus did not come
among us to change the mind
of God about us.

Jesus came to change the minds
of all of us about God.

The crucified one
must know about suffering.
God is here with us.

Forgiveness demands seeing
God in you, in me, in all.

Second Coming

All will be restored
the Alpha and Omega
union with our God

Before the Second Coming

Bear the mystery
In an imperfect cosmos
Agree to find God

An Anti-sermon

The point of His death
was not to convince us that
torture is good news.

Haiku for Jesus

−1 Don't make Jesus small,
a problem solver for sin,
a hostage - not Christ.

+1 Christ is the promise,
pioneer and perfecter,
God in human form.

−2 Don't make Jesus small,
God's plan B to rescue us,
A cipher for sins.

+2 He is the union,
Spirit coming in matter.
Christ is the alpha.

−3 Don't watch the parade.
Follow him as a partner.
Be a fisherman.

+3 From the beginning
Cosmic Christ in space and time,
our omega point

−4 Not a vague Jesus,
not just a Jesus who died
on the cross for sins

+4 Prophetic, kingdom-
of-God-love-mercy-justice-
compassion Jesus

Invitation to a Higher Place

How's the personal
salvation plan going now,
tired little mind?

No more bargaining with God,
no reward or punishment

Beyond the contract
is grace, a new covenant
of incarnation.

Come to the banquet of trust,
of mercy and steadfast love.

40 Days

He found your presence
alone in the wilderness
and gave that to us.

Untitled

Those images are
not void but begin journeys
to a deeper truth.

Must Be Crazy

"Out of his mind," his
family thought. "A danger
too," said the neighbors.

How he escaped from the cliff
after that we just don't know?

Getting Saved

When I am willing
to lose this life, I begin
to love and to live.

If I try to save my life,
Jesus says, I will lose it.

Suffering #1

Ego insists on
understanding while faith waits
on the great threshold.

Suffering #2 - from Richard Rohr

Wait on the threshold,
then stand in liminal space.
Hold the contraries,

until you are moved by grace.
Our pain is not just our own.

Cross #9

If forgiveness needs
to be paid for, then it's not
forgiveness at all.

A revelation of love ~
the cross is this or nothing.

Uprising #1

"You are the place where
I stand," he said, "on the day
when my feet are sore."

This is an Irish saying about trust, translated into English,
and in this haiku spoken by the rising Christ to all of us.
Anastasis is the Greek word at the top of the icon. It is
usually translated as *resurrection* though its literal meaning
is *uprising*.

Uprising #2

We all have a share
in this catholic uprising.
Death is defeated.

This kind of icon
goes back to the
7th century in the
Orthodox
tradition. The
rising Christ has
the wrists of
Adam and Eve -
representing all
of humanity.
There are also
other biblical
figures rising as
well. Christ is
standing on a
cross made from
the broken gates
of Hades.

Prayers

Sometimes I See

Fountain of fullness,
our world is a mirror through
which we pass to you.

Lord's Prayer

Close as the air we breathe,
our call to you is holy.
May you light our path,

and fill us with your Spirit
in this place and in these times.

You give all we need
and forgive as we forgive
the sins of others,

not in the open sea but
in the current of you love.

Prayer on Earth Day during the Easter Season

Creator of the universe,
our souls are for your blessing.
You set the cornerstone of the Earth
while the stars and angels sang.
You know where light comes from
and where darkness lives.

May we listen to your gift of the Earth.
Let our souls resonate with your call
and come alive with the greening of the world.
Let the animals teach us of your presence.

For it is not by our wisdom that
the eagle flies or the heron knows
where to build her nest. It is not
our knowledge that brings a salmon back
to the gravelly streams of its origin.

Let the rainbow remind us that
your covenant is with all life.
When you send forth your Spirit,
life appears, and you renew
the face of the Earth.

You have put us near the sea
where ships sail and orcas delight
to splash and swim,
where crabs and fish hide in eel grass
and sea birds find their food.

You have put us near mountains
with forests of fir, hemlock, and cedar,
near fields for cattle, fields producing
berries and corn to gladden our hearts.
Let bird song remind us to be thankful.

As we contemplate the birds of the air
and the lilies of the field, may we remember
that Jesus was present to everyone and everything.
The whole world is a sacrament, no collection
of objects but a communion of subjects.

Spirit of God, Risen Christ, Holy One,
in beauty your Presence is manifest,
calling us to become the wholeness you created.
You are the mighty way for everything
in the Heavens and on the Earth.
May we find our way to care for
the wonders of your continuing creation.

-from the Books of Genesis, Job, and Psalms 104 and 148

In a cross section
of SpaceTime for our wholeness
the Word became flesh.

Thanksgiving Prayer

Thank you for calling us to life.
Help our spirits to feel that calling daily.
Thank you for allowing us to share this life,
and help us not to be stingy in that sharing.
Thank you for the wonder we feel.
Help our sorrows make our joys burn brighter.
Thank you for the music of your ongoing revelation.
Help us not to fall back into the wounds we thought healed.
Thank you for being with us in our suffering.
Help us to know we never suffer apart from you.
Thank you for the others in our lives.
Keep our fears from holding us apart from all you have
made.

Waiting

As the tide recedes,
wait for a deeper seeing.
Delight in what is.

Light Fall
An Evening Prayer

For tasting the life
You have given today
and for your loving
presence,
I give thanks.

What miracles needed
my attention today?
Where was your touch
That I could share it,
Your laughter that I
could hear it?

In the morning let my mind find clarity.
Refresh my imagination.
Bring my awareness to the blessings
we share and the grace we receive.

Let the darkness come
and cares fall away.

Mathematical  Conjectures

SpaceTime

SpaceTime is sacred.
Boundaries of prayer disappear,
peace beyond knowledge.

Written June 15, 2017. I like the physics behind this.
SpaceTime has no boundaries. But not even the space
beyond the last galaxy is there. Perhaps even the space
smaller than a Planck length is not there. Unbounded and
infinite are not quite the same. If the cosmos went on
forever, our night sky would be filled with light, but we see
stars and galaxies and planets. And what of time you say?
The future surely seems unbounded. Even though we like to
think that the past has a boundary something like the Big
Bang, we can't run the laws of physics that far backward to
time zero. It seems only God is beyond this physical
understanding of the universe.

Some use the word contemplation where I use prayer here.
They say the word prayer is corrupted because some use it to
engage in the nonsensical task of trying to control God.
While I agree with this perspective, the word contemplation
comes with its own baggage, very high brow sometimes. I
use the word prayer instead of contemplation or meditation
because for me it includes these other understandings and
for purposes of haiku it has fewer syllables.

A Secular Trinity

The open rose fades; the wheel turns.
Nothing stands still.
Creation evolved us
who discovered forms describing creation.
There are three infinite worlds.
Creation from quarks to cosmos
is only the first.

"Why should there be space?"
I asked the great radiance;
"Why should there be time?"

The second world evolved in time.
Human consciousness
has no quarks or stars,
or quantum systems.
We are not stuff any universe expected.

"Why am I aware?"
I asked a passing mystic;
"Whose presence is this?"

The mathematical forms that describe creation
are discovered or created within our consciousness.
This third world maps the first;
The circle is complete, or so its seems.

Are there no other
trinities, infinities that
call us in this hour?

The call to life and to death
and rising forms a circle.

I used to believe in only
causation, symmetry, and death,
and thought grace
an inarticulate mechanism
of resurrection's impossible dream.

My beliefs are a shallow stream,
without the depth of trust and presence –
the rose fades; the wheel turns.
Nothing stands still.

Now – time is at peace.
Here – is the place where love blooms.
This – is your presence.

The Physics of Forgiveness

No thing is perfect.
Of that we have no knowledge.
Beauty is broken.

Symmetry is evidence.
Forgiveness removes the weight.

The gate of heaven
is narrow but beauty keeps
it open for us.

I would feel strange getting
there with weight still around me.

The field that is forgiveness
has darkness at one pole
and love at the other.
The shape of the field is such
that I see neither pole completely.
The darkness might be too dark,
and the love might blind me.
I look the other way.

Pray then for the grace
to forgive so I am not
swimming against the current
or misaligned like a stick
that can't get through a grate.
Going against the current,
the weight is more, yet I grow smaller.
Time heals unless I try
to keep the hurt alive.
Memory can be an obstacle,
forgetfulness a friend.

Will be aiming toward
forgiveness of everything.
Not much else makes sense.

Forgiveness is the opposite of gravity
though not quite levity.
It's orthogonal to entropy since
this field forgives the march of time.

Unbounded Images

Begin with a cube.
Remove a pair of
opposite faces.
Open to the
unbounded.
Make five more to
have a fundamental
region,
Or perhaps a region
complicated
With memories and
mirrors.

Like an infinite chessboard
Taken to another dimension,
The apeirohedron plays
With our understanding of
In and out, up and down,
Here and there, here and now.
When static becomes dynamic,
Change in one space
Effects the fabric of the whole.

Transform the points to faces
And faces to points.
The unbounded meet
At the boundary.
With each edge
The size of a Planck length
There may be space
For extra dimensions.

Some visions vanish.
These walls are not barriers.
They become a meeting place,
The end of all our exploring,
Unknowing for the first time,
A place to be both lost and
found.

Cross Purposes

Jesus taught the way
to our redemption was to
accept paradox.

To be lost is to be found;
cross purposes reconsile.

Chords at right angles,
a geometric cross finds
the circle's center.

In life share the fate of God,
and love the way that God loves.

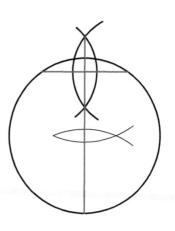

Natural World

Chinook

Here I swim where I began
feeling the current,
smelling its sweetness,
knowing life's rhythm,
called by a presence,
guarding these ova,
waiting for a big red-backed,
hook-nosed mate,
waiting for this new life,
and waiting to die.
In their deaths
my sisters and brothers
showed me how to live.

New life grows, wanders and seeks rhythms -
first light and dark
then hunger and food,
then salt and savor,
safety and danger.
Some of these ova will find
the safety of eel grass,
will watch their kind

eaten by bigger fish,
will learn to avoid
the world of the rock dogs
and the surfaces patrolled by eagles
In their deaths
my sisters and brothers
showed me how to live.

My children will find
the vast and open sea,
the bounty and the mystery,
hunger and food.
They will see many cycles
of light and dark, cold and warm
until a time in the light
when they will remember
the sweetness and long for its smell.
They will see siblings swimming with them.

The journey is complete for few.
They must know to stop eating
so they can smell home
and follow the path there,
to listen for the cry of the orca
and avoid their places,
to accept the changes in their bodies,
to enjoy the rush of a final rhythm.
Some will find this peace of living
and the grace to die.

Blackberries

In fields, vacant lots, at the edges of our property,
At the edges of our lives blackberries grow. Randomly
Their thorns inspire us to be more careful in our choices.
I met them in the summer when I was six.
They introduced themselves between laurels in the hedge.
The many shades of the berries bore witness to change.
Each shade had a different taste and feel.
Each new vantage point through the leaves a different
harvest.
Each new day a few more berries to eat.
Some harvests came with thorns.

Ed and Letti were darkly familiar.
My father's parents who had known want
Were teaching me to work.
Pick berries and don't eat them.
They came at the height of blackberry summer.
Letti had turned flour to bread
And gardens to meals.
Ed turned coal to power and iron to steel.
Now they brought a new view to my berries,
Picked and processed – to leave them would be a sin.

The overgrown terraces on the hillside
Behind the laurel hedge gave us
Places to stand to pick bucket after bucket.
Berries were crushed in cheesecloth
And hung on every knob in the kitchen.
Berry juice became jelly – so much we never finished it all.
Ed's passing, a new house, another August,
Boards that held concrete and
Would become a shed for animals
Temporarily my ramp to the best berries.
A place in space, seven feet above the ground,
Held there by the strength of the vines
And my own sense of balance.
It would have been a rough fall
Into the blackberry thorns.
My brothers were there too, eating the berries
Closer to the ground.
But they wanted the challenge too – the thorns will hurt;
Don't lean over too far; put the board back.
We had enough that day.
There would be more days, a few thorns,
Lots of blackberries.

A decade of Augusts turned to Septembers.
Still many ripe blackberries
To contribute to the commonweal.
Many friends eating, talking, picking
On the edge of a farm field.

We made wine with most of them.
Thorns were not expected.
The containers exploded in October,
And there was a mess in the basement.
It blew up on us – the wine,
The commune, the lifestyle.

Yesterday I took my grandson Eddie
To the blackberry patch in the alley.
He liked the berries and will be back.
He likes the cobbler too
Even if I add my Grandpa John's rhubarb.

Today I startled a mother and daughter
As I went to pick in the vacant lot behind our house.
The little girl said I needed some berries in my bowl.
She went to another part of the bramble
And returning put a handful of berries in my bowl.
They were gone before I could say thank you.

Tomorrow when I see blackberry pickers wander by
I'll stay inside and wait my turn.
Picking blackberries is a simple chore.
The manifest was hidden,
But we have seen it.

Osprey

On a spar where eagles usually perch
An osprey watched us and the seascape
In the waning light of early May.
Do you prefer patterns of the dark?
Are you looking
To the freedom of the night
When no eagles will come?

Do you look to a new beginning?
This is only the surface.
We are not alone.
We eat food, make plans and dream.
I get lost in relationships, not always a bad thing.
But sometimes I forget who I am.
Better than I know mine, you know your heart.
But a presence knows us too
Patterned with light and dark as we are,
Even when I wear the wrong clothes
Or fall out of belonging to what is before me.
Can we let the thoughts of the day move on
So we are left with only the presence?
As we watch this day pass
May we also find our real selves
Before sleep takes us to the next light.

Red November

I was walking on a path on Semiahmoo shore listening to Keith Jarrett's Koln Concert, the concert on broken piano for a young producer who cried. Part 1 of the solo piano had already set the mood by making the SpaceTime boundaries of my soul seem as large as all the beaches I've walked on and as long as my whole life. Tears were in my eyes too.

Dune grass gave way to wild rose bushes. Red birds (house finches) stayed on the wild roses until I could almost touch them. Then in a rush of fluttering and swooping flew off to some further bushes and the eagle perches. A few more meters down the gravel path to another rose bush and the whole fluttering happened again and still again from a bush on the other side of the path. I noticed the red rose hips, perhaps the reason for the congregating in the first place. Upon my passing the last rose bush, one last finch flew up then back to a small pine four times, and then hid from me in the pine. Was the bird annoyed with me for ending the gathering? Was this last flight for my entertainment? Could some of the rose hips have been fermented, and this last finch have become a little tipsy?

My mother told me about sitting in her backyard with her cousin and watching birds getting drunk on naturally fermented berries in the late Minnesota spring. Birds fell out of the bushes and flopped around the lawn. The girls laughed and rolled around the lawn themselves. Her cousin thought these were the best birds ever.

As I passed another hiker walking the other way on the beach, I wanted to leave the gravel path when I could find a way down to the beach for my return. Keith Jarrett was finishing Part 1 as I walked the first few steps on beach gravel. Just off shore ducks, coots, and mergansers were feeding. I synchronized their feeding dives as I walked by. A single seagull didn't seem to care that I passed as I didn't give him a second look either. I was looking for special stones in the beach gravel, stones that has fascinated me since childhood. White agates and the various grays of granite seemed to form patterns though I knew their placement by the waves was completely random.

On the way home I saw a pair of eagles circling high in the air. Later I got to see my first winter flock of sanderlings, flashing their white bellies in their circus flights. This was the best outing of the year for an older man in this red and gray and white November.

Awake and aware,
one sees clearly with the heart.
Not yet, already

Photo Sources

CPSIA information can be obtained
at www.ICGtesting.com
Printed in the USA
LVHW072353050220
646038LV00013B/557